UNDERSTANDING

YOUR HORSE

Schüssler Tissue Salts
for Horses

UNDERSTANDING
YOUR HORSE

HANS-HEINRICH JOERGENSEN

Schüssler Tissue Salts for Horses

Healthy and fit
with minerals

Copyright © 2007 by Cadmos Verlag GmbH, Brunsbek
Design: Ravenstein + Partner, Verden
Typesetting: Nadine Hoenow
Title Photo: Christiane Slawik/Anneke Bosse
Photos: Anneke Bosse, Deutsche Homeopathie-Union,
Hans-Heinrich Joergensen, Mineraliensammlung Berthold
Weber, Christiane Slawik, Tierklinik Sottrum
Edited by Anneke Bosse
Translated by Ute Weyer
Print: LVDM, Linz

Printed in Austria

ISBN 978-3-86127-926-6

Contents

Contents

Biochemistry—what is it?
Therapy with Schüssler tissue salts

"Biochemistry" is no miracle cure that can fix everything that the vets have tried in vain to put right. Nor is it a form of esoteric therapy that one has to believe in in order to get results. Biochemistry is just a natural form of treatment, based on scientific knowledge.

When homeotherapist and general practitioner Dr Heinrich Schüssler first published his ideas about a specific mineral therapy in a medical journal in 1873, he was well ahead of his time. Despite being a general practitioner and homeopath, however, his advanced ideas were not particularly popular amongst his colleagues.

Confronted by the ignorance of his fellow doctors, who stubbornly followed the conventional medical practices of the previous century, and who laughed at his unorthodox ideas, Schüssler wrote a short article about his thoughts regarding this new treatment, introducing it to the broader public and to patients.

Soon, there was an upsurge of interest in the benefits of homeopathic mineral therapy, and vets began to take an interest in it too.

The first veterinary surgeons to actively promote and advocate Schüssler's mineral therapy were two of his fellow Germans, Doctors Grashorn and Meinert. In 1902, Dr Meinert founded the Biochemical Union, which so far has survived a century, two world wars, five governments and five currencies.

Frustrated by consistently unsuccessful conventional treatment methods, Dr Meinert began to explore alternative therapies, and came across Schüssler's document. He stated: "I studied this short document carefully and was impressed by its clarity and simplicity." After successfully treating his own illnesses as well as those of his family, he applied the principles to animals, which rekindled his passion for the veterinary profession.

At length he summarised his experience in a "Guide to Biochemical Treatment of Domestic Animals," which was widely distributed at the time and again published more recently in 1996 by Friedrich Bartel-

Eine

Abgekürzte Therapie.

Anleitung zur biochemischen Behandlung der Krankheiten

von

Dr. med. Schüßler.

Fünfundzwanzigste, theilweise umgearbeitete Auflage.

Oldenburg und Leipzig, 1898.
Schulze'sche Hof-Buchhandlung und Hof-Buchdruckerei.
(A. Schwartz.)

Schüssler's "Short Therapy" explains his thoughts about mineral treatment and provoked interest from patients, doctors and vets.

meyer, who produced a new edition. This rewarding small book can be purchased through the Biochemical Union for, as can the original document by Schüssler.

Sometimes, the simpler a successful new idea is, the harder it can seem to understand it. Schüssler's approach was to research what inorganic minerals actually do to a human or animal organism.

Organic chemistry consists of the elements of nitrogen (N), oxygen (O),

Veterinarians soon realised that animals could only be truly healthy if a supply of minerals is assured. (Photo: Slawik)

carbon (C) and hydrogen (H). We know now that life based on these elements alone is not possible, and that numerous inorganic elements enable and control essential metabolic processes. The chemistry of life, biochemistry, describes the permanent interaction of elementary chemical processes.

Wilhelm Heinrich Schüssler was one of the first scientists to attempt to understand these fundamental interactions, and to find out which elements trigger certain reactions and which diseases develop if a link in one of these chains is missing. Schüssler created the expression "biochemistry", and it has now become a commonly used medical definition to describe exactly what Schüssler set out to investigate: the understanding of cell metabolism. It is unfortunate that many modern biochemists have forgotten the name Schüssler.

Of course, conventional medicine also uses mineral treatment. Many dedicated groups now research the effects of minerals, plenty of literature is published on a continuous basis and there are at least five highly specialised conferences every year that talk exclusively about biochemistry. The incentive for conventional medicine to pay attention to minerals and trace elements actually originates from veterinary science. Vets were early to recognise that the performance of animals is closely linked to their mineral metabolism.

The tissue salts that Schüssler regarded as crucial in order to sustain life are precisely those that modern medicine also declares to be essential. These are the elements calcium, potassium, magnesium, sodium, ferrum and silicea, in connection with the anions phosphate, sulphur and chloride, and in particular, Schüssler's favourite salt, fluoride. Schüssler called his salts "functional remedies" because they are vital for physiological processes and metabolism.

Nowadays, these functions are well researched and understood. We know that potassium has a calming effect on the nervous system, whilst sodium stimulates nerve impulses. Calcium is essential for muscle contractions; magnesium is essential to help enzymes maintain a biological balance.

Usually, quite minimal amounts are effective—and for that reason, Schüssler applied his salts in homeopathic concentrations. However, Schüssler never administered his remedies on the basis of Hahnemann's homeopathic principles, but instead used homeopathic potencies in order to achieve a maximum effect. He created a modern expression that is now employed heavily in the pharmaceutical industry: bioavailability. An oral medication is of no use if it passes straight through the intestinal tract and is not available for metabolic processes. The break-down of a substance into the smallest particles increases the active surface area, at least with substances that are not soluble in water (more on page 21).

This book cannot replace the vet! It can, however, help you to understand how to apply some first aid and self-help solutions while you are waiting for the vet to arrive, and also to support any veterinary treatment. Many minor ailments can be successfully and cheaply treated with Schüssler salts. Of course, a horse-owner is faced with the decision of whether the applied treatment is all that is required, or if the vet has to be consulted. The better you know your horse, the easier this decision will be.

Humans and animals require only the smallest amounts of many minerals in order to stay fit and healthy. (Photo: Slawik)

*Heinrich Wilhelm Schüss-
ler—a man who knew what
he wanted and who dedicated
his life to helping others.*

Who was
Dr Schüssler?
A different view of life

"Who was Schüssler?" A frequently asked question about the doctor of whom the Germans are so proud. He was born in 1821 in Bad Zwischenahn, now a popular and well-presented small tourist town in north-west Germany. His family was from a middle class background and his father worked as a civil servant, his uncle was a doctor, the older brother training to be a lawyer. Young Wilhelm had access to good education and presumably had a happy early childhood. Things changed dramatically, however, when Wilhelm was about 12 or 13 years old. It appears his father was found to have embezzled some money and he was sentenced to five years in prison.

The family was left almost penniless, and his mother took Wilhelm and his younger siblings to a poor part of the town of Oldenburg, where she struggled to feed them by cleaning, sewing and laundering. The brother at university was unable to contribute in any way. Young Schüssler had to leave school and help his mother.

The poverty, dramatic change of lifestyle, loss of friends, home, security and diminished social standing all had a deep and lasting effect on Schüssler's personality. He became cautious, sensitive and ready to fight.

Not much is known about Schüssler's early adult years. He was listed as a language teacher in Oldenburg at the age of 27, and his father, by then released from prison, worked as a music teacher. Both were just temporary jobs and not well paid. The family was still poor and constantly on the move.

The struggle for education

Evening classes as we know them today were not available then; those who wished to gain educational and academic qualifications later in life had to work much harder than their younger colleagues. Wilhelm Schüssler had to follow many difficult paths before he could open his doctor's surgery in Old-

enburg. His ability to bypass formalities, and his vigilance, certainly helped him to achieve this.

His biggest hindrance was his lack of formal school qualifications, namely the Abitur, or school matriculation. In those days, however, this were not always mandatory in order to gain entry to university, and foreign students in particular were often admitted to courses without formal qualifications. This may account for Wilhelm's starting university in Paris in 1852. In 1853, however, he changed to Berlin, and in 1854 he moved again, to Giessen, where he gained his doctor's degree a year later.

Unfortunately, all university records from Giessen were destroyed during the war, so the actual course of events by which Schüssler qualified as a doctor is by no means certain. Although a PhD was normally a mandatory requirement to qualify, it was possible to receive the medical qualification without a PhD under the obligation that a PhD was taken at a later stage. Again, Schüssler may have managed to bypass the regulations.

Registered in Giessen as a foreigner, he applied to be granted his medical qualification before the obligatory four years of study were completed, on the basis that he would serve as a military doctor with the Prussian forces, at that time preparing for possible mobilization in the Crimean War with Russia. His application was successful and he became a doctor even without a dissertation. He was in good company: Justus Liebig and Johann Wolfgang Goethe were also granted qualifications in the same way from Giessen University.

Despite all this, Schüssler was still not granted the necessary qualification to work as a medical practitioner. Academic qualifications had been granted by the university, but permission to work as a doctor was given by the government. A long exchange of letters followed, and Schüssler was eventually required to re-sit the missing Abitur. His plea to allow him to register without this qualification, or at least to sit only a restricted number of papers was not accepted; in the end, however, he passed the exams.

The next hurdle was the missing fourth university year, which he eventually completed in Prague. At long last, however, he stood in front of the critical examination board for his final exams. There are various rumours about the results. Schüssler's enemies stated that the board let him pass on the promise that he would only work as a homeopathic doctor. His supporters praised him wholeheartedly. Both are incorrect, as evidence of his results still exists.

Despite achieving only very average results, Schüssler became a successful doctor. He died a wealthy man and he once stated in a publication that he had around 12,000 consultations per year, a quite remarkable figure!

Schüssler and homeopathy

Homeopathic medicine became popular because of its gentle approach, as opposed to the crude methods of bloodletting, purging, use of morphine and chemicals then common in conventional medicine that often did more harm than good. Schüssler practised for 17 years using homeopathic methods. However, even in his early publications, and despite writing a homeopathic teaching book, it became apparent that the homeopathic principles did not satisfy him completely. He did not follow Hahnemann's laws of "treating like with like", but applied "Contraria contrariis", treatment with an antidote.

Schüssler did not prescribe medication according to the picture the illness presented, but tried to find specific drugs for certain diseases.

Many modern homeopaths do this as well, although they might not admit this deviation from traditional homeopathic rules. Schüssler, however, discussed this openly. There are documents about a scientific argument as to whether applied remedies can produce symptoms in healthy people, or whether, as Schüssler insisted, these bring out a disease that was already latent. A sacrilege for homeopaths as it means that the disease is already there; the drug only activates it.

As early as 1862, long before the development of his biochemistry, Schüssler started into looking for deficiencies: "What is the substance that, when lacking or insufficient, will cause the disease?" It seems clear that he had arrived at a different viewpoint regarding the causes of illnesses and their treatment, which subsequently led to a very new approach in his medicine.

The following quote further demonstrates his departure from the strict homeopathic laws towards allopathic thinking:

"The basic characteristics of magnesia salts are the same, but magnesium phosphate works faster…"

I feel this quote confirms my own view of the effect of biochemical remedies. Firstly, it is important to be aware of the effects potassium, calcium, magnesium, etc. have on the body. The differences between remedy No 4 (potassium chloride), No 5 (potassium phosphate) and No 6 (potassium sulphate) are significant, but nevertheless secondary.

Because of constant arguments, Schüssler finally resigned from the committee of homeopathic practitioners; this did not prevent him from donating a large sum of money to Berlin University to endow a degree course in homeopathy. The experience of his own difficult career made him plead for giving students without the Abitur and without completing the full medical course the chance to work as purely homeopathic doctors. This eventually led to the acknowledgement of the profession of homeotherapist.

cal that an organic substance should have a stronger affinity to an organic body. Nevertheless, this is not so. All minerals are inorganic, even in plants, and also in humans. That is not a matter of properties but purely of definition.

The ongoing controversies did more harm than good. Schüssler did not actually say that he was able to heal every disease with his twelve salts. His frequently criticised quote speaks of "every curable disease". His subsequent treatments have long put that into perspective.

No one doubts any more that a fractured leg needs calcium, but maybe not in the form of tablet No 12 rather than as a cast around the broken leg.

Biochemistry

The more Schüssler investigated the path of diseases caused by deficiencies, the further he moved away from homeopathic laws, which later impeded acceptance of his theories. Homeopaths could not accept his ideas, and conventional practitioners did not take him seriously.

Schüssler made life difficult for himself too, and hindered his biochemistry theory from being accepted. Even with his supporters he could take offence for trifling reasons; he was stubborn, sharp and defensive, aspects of his highly sensitive and damaged personality.

His opponents talked of a nonsense-theory, based on the assumption that the human body is unable to utilise inorganic minerals, only organic ones. Admittedly, it might seem more logi-

Outsider or scientist?

While developing his tissue salt theory, or biochemistry, Schüssler could not escape his homeopathic roots. His homeopathic background showed in particular in the preparation of his salts which, although meant as supplements, were prepared in homeopathic potencies (see page 21 onwards). The reason was not the energy transfer, but improvement of bioavailability, a concept that is now widely used in the pharmaceutical industry. The high dilution is compensated by a breakdown into the tiniest particles, such that a D6 potency can achieve more than one millionth of a gram of substance. If we have doubts about the efficacy of these high potencies, e.g. the

Schüssler was often criticised for his supposed statement that he could cure any ailment with his twelve salts—in fact he never actually claimed that.
(Photo: Slawik)

"Hot Seven"—ten tablets of magnesium phosphate dissolved in hot water—we can use a D3 or even the original substance. Schüssler did not insist on using a D6, and he used lower potencies as well.

It became more and more apparent that Schüssler considered his salts as supplements for lacking minerals, and less as homeopathic remedies. Even nowadays, biochemists have difficulties with this theory, and the arguments continue. In modern biochemical literature, homeopathic and allopathic principles are randomly used, which adds further to the confusion.

I always make a clear distinction between homeopathic principles and pure supplementation. This does not

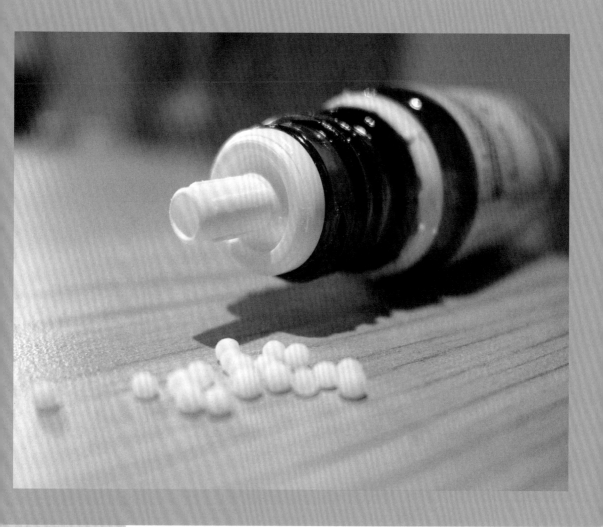

There are significant diffe-rences between how homeopa-thic remedies (left) and Schüssler tissue salts (right) act on the body, even if both are used at high potencies. (Photos: Bosse)

mean that we have to choose between these concepts; both are effective. We have to, however, be clear about which treatment is based on homeopathy and which is supplementary. This is essen-tial in order to give biochemical treat-ments the deserved credit and also in order to properly licence these reme-dies under pharmaceutical legislation, which distinguishes between homeop-athy and allopathy. There is nothing in between, and medications that do not fall into one of these two categories dis-appear off the market.

Allopathy is not a swear word even if some of its principles are open to question. No one would want to forgo modern medicine in serious cases. Schüssler's medicine was modern med-icine at the time. He was one of the

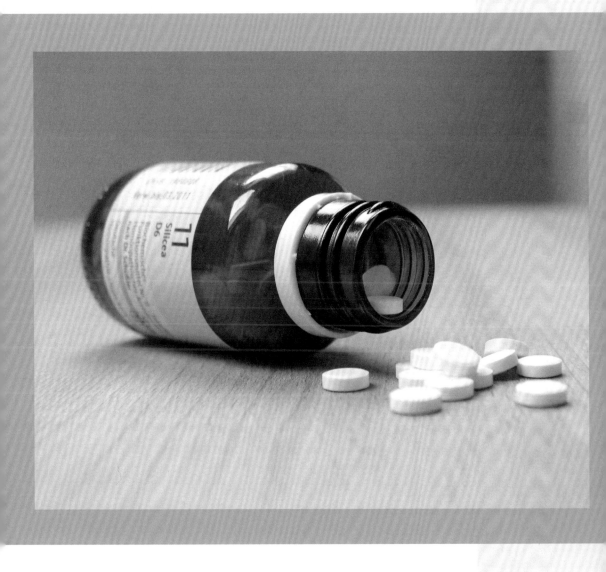

few, like Liebig, Virchow or Mole-schott, who wanted to advance medicine from the orthodox approaches of his time, to open-minded science. He asked himself what actually happens in a cell, what does it require for its metabolism and which substances act where and how.

Schüssler created the term "biochemistry", the chemistry of life, in order to demonstrate clearly at what his therapy is aimed. This definition is now widely used in medicine, but in Schüssler's time it was called physical chemistry. Schüssler's and the current academic ideas of biochemistry are similar: both investigate and research metabolism with the aim of helping sick people. However, we should not think of biochemistry purely in

Schüssler's terms, as it has long been a fixed part of modern medicine.

Schüssler spent his whole life looking for the correct way forward. He constantly questioned his own theories and revised them, as can be seen in the 26th edition of his "Short Therapy".

Schüssler tried to get acknowledgement for his theories and help and support from colleagues. Therefore, we should not simply accept his concepts but continue to develop them further in parallel with modern medicine.

Many a biochemist is unaware that Schüssler's idea of treatment with minerals has long been a widely accepted part of modern medicine. There should be more interaction between both groups, because modern medicine can benefit from the 130 years of practical experience of the biochemists, and the Schüssler group can profit from current research and knowledge.

Whenever I look at a picture of Schüssler I see a face used to fighting, with a touch of the defensiveness that accompanied him all his life. I also see a face of a person eager to help others, during his life and beyond. In his will, he made generous provision to establish a charitable foundation that would "support poor and helpless people of all beliefs and religions," further stipulating that "No invoices from my medical records should be raised and no one should know who has paid and who hasn't." For Schüssler, it was not about money, it was all about helping people, a good philosophy for any doctor. That was Schüssler!

Small Doses — Big Effects

Dr Hahnemann's homeopathic concept

More than half a century before Schüssler, there had already been a fundamental change in classical medicine. Samuel Hahnemann, a German practitioner, had developed homeopathy. It was based on his idea of treating diseases not with an antidote, but with a remedy that creates the very symptoms of the illness, and which is given in a very highly diluted form, in order to heal the symptoms. This principle was termed similia similibus curentur— "like cures like".

Hahnemann's model was based on an assumed vital energy that needs to be corrected, and therefore homeopaths speak about the energetic, rather than pharmacological effects of their remedies.

They do not talk about dilution, but potentiation, based on the idea that a remedy is stronger the higher the potency is. In order to create a decimal potency, the pure substance of plant, animal or mineral origin is mixed with nine parts of lactose or diluted in nine parts of alcohol.

The treatment of the homeopathic potency

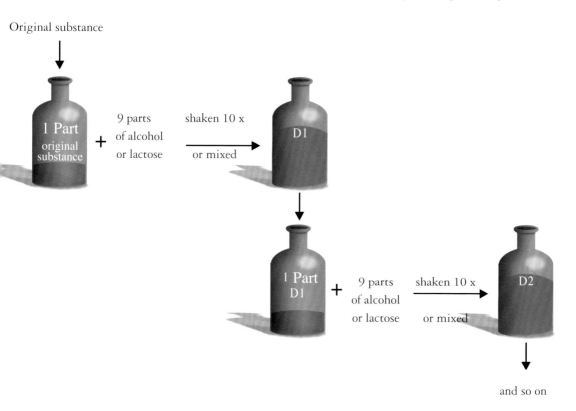

Original substance

1 Part original substance + 9 parts of alcohol or lactose — shaken 10 x or mixed → D1

1 Part D1 + 9 parts of alcohol or lactose — shaken 10 x or mixed → D2

and so on

You then produce the potency D1. If you repeat the process using D1, you will get a D2, and so forth. If you started with one gram of the original substance, you will find only one millionth of a part, one microgram, in an equivalent volume of potency D6.

With lower potencies, one can still assume a primarily pharmacological effect of the remedy. After all, milligram (D3) and microgram (D6) are dosages that are also used in conventional medicine.

Scientists, however, argue that with high potencies beyond D23, no single molecule of the original substance is present any more, although homeopaths claim that the energy information of the substance is still transmitted and has even become stronger.

Homeopathic information or mineral supplement?

The argument about the efficacy of Schüssler's tissue salts has been ongoing for generations. Do they follow the homeopathic principle of correction of imbalances, or do they work as a mineral supplement? This continuing discussion stems from doubts as to whether such a minute amount of substance, as in a D6 or D12 potency, can actually have pharmacological properties.

In a recent paper in a well-known scientific journal, a committed biochemist further questioned this. He calculated that in order to extract one gram of iron ore, one would need 80,000 lorry loads of ferrum phosphate D12. However, we only require about ten micrograms to treat minor insufficiencies, and if we use a D6 instead of a D12 we would only need two tins of iron.

Since we are talking about Schüssler's biochemistry rather than the views of his critics, I would like to cite a few sentences from the last edition of Schüssler's book. Even then, Schüssler was confronted with scepticism that such high potencies could be effective:

" Nature works only with atoms and molecules."

"There can be no doubt that minute, not measurable amounts of substance have an effect on an organism."

"The mineral content of a cell is minuscule .... Allopathic remedies work in small dosages too."

"... how small must a dose of magnesia be that is effective against neuralgia which is caused by the tiniest of deficits of the mineral in a minute part of the nervous tissue?"

This emphasises that we do not require huge amounts to treat a deficit. Each deficit starts with a tiny amount and in order to cure this we do not have to supplement the full daily requirement but only that small deficit, so that a cell can resume its normal function.

If we do not attempt to fill ourselves up with supplements but instead follow a healthy diet and only treat a specific deficit and also use a D6 instead of D12, then we only require a dose or two of ferrum phosphate, not 80,000 lorry loads:

"... may every practitioner who uses biochemical remedies choose the required dosage as he sees fit."

As we know from letters to his chemist, Schüssler often used lower potencies too. We have to ask ourselves whether a lower potency and therefore a higher amount of substance, is sometimes more indicated. For treatment of horses, I personally will always use a D6, instead of the D12 potency recommended for humans, and rather than the human D6 I would give a horse a D3.

If we take more tablets instead of using a lower potency, we will certainly increase the amount of substance, but most of all, we increase the amount of lactose. In order to achieve a stronger effect, however, we should follow Hahnemann's principle and use a higher potency.

Although an experienced homeopath, Schüssler always emphasised that his salts were not homeopathic remedies. According to the "like cures like" rule, a lack of calcium for example would not be an indication for applying calcium phosphate, but rather a calcium poisoning or an illness that displays those symptoms.

Schüssler made clear he chose homeopathic preparations of the salts not because of energy principles, but because of a better bioavailability:

"All hydrophobic substances have to be diluted at least up to the sixth potency; all hydrophilic substances are able to pass the cell membranes in lower potencies."

Organic minerals

Again and again, one comes across the absurd idea that the human body is unable to metabolise inorganic minerals, and that they could block cells and vessels; and that a person who needs organic minerals should drink distilled water in order to unblock the cells.

Just to make a point: the expression "organic minerals" is a contradiction in itself. All minerals are inorganic. That is not a matter of effect, quality

or origin, but of definition. The positively charged cations sodium, calcium, potassium and magnesium, in combination with the negatively charged anions chloride, phosphate and sulphate, have been used in biochemistry for 130 years.

Minerals retain their "inorganic" properties even when embedded in plants or a human body.

This does not compromise their efficiency; on the contrary, their electrophysical properties are responsible for regulating nerve and muscle impulses and fluid and energy metabolism.

The anions and cations can, however, find and bond organic substances too, for example lactate, orotate or gluconate. There is no evidence that these combinations are metabolised any better. There is more evidence to the contrary, because these molecules are larger and the bonding with the cation even more stable. The theory that such a combination with an organic anion would penetrate a cell easier is contrary to all physiological knowledge. Absorption through the intestinal membranes is regulated by the metabolic situation of the body: if there is a lack, the absorption rates increase, and vice versa decrease in case of a surplus.

The minerals are also called electrolytes, because of the electrical charges that separate them. Potassium chloride divides into potassium on one side and chloride on the other. Each biochemical activity of an electrolyte is based on its separation from its reactive partner (ionisation), and it unfolds its vital energy while searching for a

As "organic" as an organism may be, nevertheless it cannot exist without "inorganic" minerals. (Photo: Slawik)

new one, a process that is independent of the former partner.

If, as some claim, the body was incapable of eliminating inorganic minerals, this would lead to the organism turning into a salt lake. Our kidneys are well equipped to eliminate minerals, and they also prevent a mineral overload by checking the blood concentration and excreting any surplus.

Distilled water

Your washing machine might prefer soft, demineralised water, but your heart and your horse like hard water, full of minerals and rich in "inorganic" combinations. If you want your washing machine to outlive you then you should drink distilled water, but otherwise you are able to supply your body with significant amounts of calcium and magnesium from your drinking water, which can prevent heart attack and mineral deficiencies.

The calcium and magnesium content in water determines its hardness, and is measured in °d. One degree (1°d) corresponds to 10 milligrams of calcium oxide or 7.19 milligrams of magnesium oxide per litre of water. A water of 12°d hardness, an average value, supplies your horse with about 1 gram of magnesium daily. The electrical conductivity of water is determined by the diluted electrolytes. The fewer electrolytes present, the lower the conductivity, or the higher the electrical resistance, expressed in ohms.

Dosage and application

Biochemists advise their human patients not to swallow the tablets, but to let them dissolve in their mouth. If several remedies are necessary, they should be taken separately, because some have an antagonistic effect. Although they mix well when in the blood stream, some can disturb each other before they are absorbed.

Some horses will happily eat the sweet tablets, but you can also dissolve them in water and syringe them into its mouth.
(Photo: Bosse)

If the tablets which contain such minute amounts of substance are swallowed, they have to pass through the oesophagus, the stomach, the intestines, the liver vessels and liver before they are dissolved into the blood and available to the organism. The so-called first pass effect avoids this long journey by reaching the blood stream via the membranes of the mouth.

It is of course impossible to teach most horses to dissolve tablets in their mouth. Therefore we have to give a higher dose to compensate for the loss of substance during passaging.

The golden rule for humans is to take one tablet three times a day, dissolved in the mouth. A horse should be given seven to ten tablets three times daily. Some horses are very fussy and will not eat the tablets with their feed. In this case, you can dissolve them in water and syringe them straight into the muzzle. Make sure you lift the horse's head for a moment to prevent the mixture from running out of the mouth again.

100 tablets?

One group of human practitioners considers the application of seven to eight Schüssler salts at the same time, ten tablets per salt three times daily, to be essential. That way you will create a soup of lactose that replaces your dinner, but this has nothing to do with Schüssler's biochemistry. Following this approach, you would feed your horse lactose rather than oats!

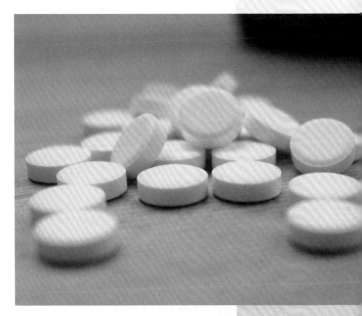

It's not about the quantity! Each insufficiency starts with a tiny amount, therefore small doses can have a big effect. (Photo: Bosse)

Although Schüssler's therapy is not based on the homeopathic "like cures like" principle but on correcting deficiencies, the above-mentioned method is illogical. If you doubt the effectiveness of a D6 potency (0.0000025 gram per tablet), you can use a D3 (0.0025 gram) instead of administering ten or more tablets. The smaller the D number the higher is the substance content.

Even some of the most enthusiastic biochemists doubt the effectiveness of such small amount of substance, although a D3 operates in the region of milligrams and a D6 of micrograms, which are certainly dosages used in conventional medicine as well. Each insufficiency starts slowly, and these remedies are not meant to replace a full daily requirement but merely to correct small imbalances. They cannot and should not substitute a healthy diet rich in minerals.

Marble, stone, iron ...
The twelve functional remedies

Originally, Dr Schüssler listed his twelve functional remedies differently. Later, someone put them into alphabetical order and numbered them. They are now known as such and can often be referred to just by their number.

Only No 12 is out of place: Schüssler eventually excluded calcium sulphate, which he no longer considered to be essential. His followers, however, kept it.

The twelve functional remedies

1:	Calcium fluoride
2:	Calcium phosphate
3:	Ferrum phosphate
4:	Potassium chloride
5:	Potassium phosphate
6:	Potassium sulphate
7:	Magnesium phosphate
8:	Sodium chloride
9:	Sodium phosphate
10:	Sodium sulphate
11:	Silicea
12:	Calcium sulphate

The Biochemical Union in Germany supplies everyone who is interested with a free brochure explaining the full indications of all twelve salts. I want to concentrate on the main effects used for equine treatment and on those that are now recognised by allopathic medicine too.

When you study the therapeutic concepts of other alternative medicines you will notice that they too use biochemistry. For example, all plant materials that are used to treat deterioration of bones, tendons and joints have a very high silicea content—silicea (Schüssler's No 11) is the classical remedy against such ailments.

Rudolph Steiner's anthroposophy uses Schüssler's minerals as well, under different names, for example quartz instead of silicea or sylvite instead of potassium chloride. These are the names of the stones that contain the minerals.

I am not a friend of alphabetical lists of diseases that then suggest the relevant drugs for quick treatments. It is far more important that one understands the properties and indications of each remedy and also recognises what is wrong with a horse. This will more or less inevitably lead to the right choice of treatment. Therefore, you will find numerous indications in the description of each tissue salt and many tips when discussing horses' problems. Try and understand the concept—that will get you on the right path.

No 1: Calcium fluoride

No 1, calcium fluoride, is usually applied at a D12 potency in human homeopathy.

An electron-microscopic image of calcium fluoride. (Photo: Deutsche Homöopathie-Union)

Conventional medicine also uses fluoride combinations for treatment of osteoporosis and as a preventative for dental caries, but in concentrations that would equate to a homeopathic D2, close to the toxic limits.

I came across a recommendation to use a D3 on the Internet which I found frightening. Fluoride is an essential trace element, but really only as a trace. In higher concentrations, it is a highly potent cell toxin and should be administered with the greatest caution.

Apatite, a substance found in bones, is a calcium-fluoride-phosphate combination. The small amount of fluoride in apatite hardens the bone substance. At one time, many practitioners prescribed fluoride to osteoporosis patients in order to prevent further demineralisation of their bones. The dosages, however, were far too high,

which led to the bones becoming too hard and brittle, and this caused a higher fracture rate. Often, school children are still treated with such high and almost toxic amounts of fluoride as a caries prophylaxis. The non-toxic D12 dilution would be completely sufficient in these cases. When treating your horse, do not use a lower potency than D6.

No 2: Calcium phosphate

Calcium phosphate, Schüssler's No 2, is far more efficient than the fluoride combinations. Humans are traditionally treated with a D6; for horses I prefer a D3.

One of its best-known properties is its ability to bind with water and

An electron-microscopic image of calcium phosphate. (Photo: Deutsche Homöopathie-Union)

Calcium is important not only for healthy bones but also to promote blood clotting after small bites or kick wounds in the field. (Photo: Slawik)

become a very hard substance, as used in mortar. Mineralisation with calcium hardens our bones and enables us to walk upright instead of crawling on the floor.

A life-long supply of calcium is most important for any horse, not just the young ones.

Therefore, greatest attention has to be paid to providing the correct amount of calcium in the diet as it is easy for mistakes to be made. The calcium supply cannot be replaced easily and has to be provided through the food or mineral supplements, although biochemistry can help correct imbalances and improve distribution. Treatment of calcium-related problems is best attempted with a combination of No 2 (calcium phosphate) and No 1 (calcium fluoride), especially for healing fractures, fissures or as prophylaxis in at-risk patients.

Calcium is important not only for bones; it also regulates many processes in the blood and muscles, and can be very helpful against a range of problems. Blood clotting, for exampling, is largely dependent on calcium distribution. Frequent haematomas (bruises) can be a sign of calcium deficit. These are difficult to spot in a horse and are often only detectable as small and painful swellings. Horses kept in a field can suffer haematomas when playing, kicking or biting or running into each other, and even after insect bites. A badly fitted saddle, or use of spurs, can also lead to bruises and pressure sores.

Calcium seals blood vessels and used to be the number one treatment for allergies. It is still very effective with all allergies unless the allergy is accompanied by severe swelling of the airways and requires emergency treatment. The injected poison of an insect bite causes histamine release, with swelling and itching. Calcium seals the membranes and will provide relief. I would also administer No 21 (zinc chloride) as additional treatment.

Calcium needs to be present in order to allow a muscle, be it a heart or skeletal muscle, to contract. Calcium is beneficial for an old horse with a weak heart and also in cases of performance problems without any other obvious cause.

Oxytocine is a hormone responsible for uterine contractions during labour. Calcium increases its effect and can be useful as an additional impulse if the labour stops prematurely. It can also help in cases of afterbirth retention, but you should never wait for more than half an hour.

No 3: Ferrum phosphate

Iron has the unfortunate ability to bind with oxygen, which is strictly

An electron-microscopic image of ferrum phosphate. (Photo: Mineraliensammlung Bertold Weber)

speaking an energy transfer, but we call it rusting. Blood contains a lot of iron for that very reason. Haemoglobin is a blood-based iron-protein combination. In the lungs, red blood cells bind oxygen and transport it through the blood vessels to areas where carbohydrates are burnt as energy supply. Blood-borne oxygen transport and exchange are impossible without iron.

Anaemia, or lack of iron, will inevitably reduce performance.

When a muscle has to work hard, local oxygen is quickly depleted and the energy supply then depends on anaerobic fuelling. This is less economical, produces less energy and leaves lactate, because additional oxygen is taken from the intercellular fluid instead of from the blood. To simplify this: one carbon atom C "burns" in combination with two oxygen atoms (O_2) and becomes CO_2. If the carbon has to use fluid-based oxygen (H_2O), each carbon atom leaves four hydrogen atoms (H^+) that can then form aggressive acids.

Essential iron cannot be supplemented biochemically; its main source for a horse is from a balanced diet. Number 3, ferrum phosphate, has predominantly anti-inflammatory properties, and even the smallest amounts are effective. Phagocytes (cleaning cells) that kill bacteria and viruses and other foreign bodies are unable to eliminate a bacterium unless they have free iron ions and free oxygen radicals available. Here you see that even free radicals are not all bad, and they do indeed fulfil a function. Free iron ions

are also able to bind bacterial toxins, which helps reduce and improve inflammatory processes.

Nos 4, 5, 6: Three potassium combinations

We use three potassium combinations in biochemistry, each of which has specific properties that I will explain in more detail later. The classical potassium property, however, is common to all three combinations: potassium is essential for the acid/base balance and for nerve function. The resting potential of a nerve cell, i.e. the threshold before it actually reacts to a stimulus, is dependent on a sufficient intracellular potassium concentration. Its internal concentration of potassium is about forty times higher than outside the cell. The potassium cations try to equalise the inner and outer concentrations and aim to escape through the cell membrane, but they are bonded to an anion, which is too big to pass through the membrane. The positive outer potassium ions stick to the outer cell membrane, and many negatively charged anions lie on the inside. This creates an electrical field that determines the resting threshold.

During an action potential, i.e. a moving exchange of ions along the nerve, the electrical field discharges. Potassium ions stream out of the cell, but at the same time so many sodium ions flow in that the inner cell becomes positive.

Good nerves are important for any major show. The potassium combinations can be very helpful here. (Photo: Slawik)

In order for an action potential to occur, the sodium channels, normally closed, have to be opened, and this happens with the help of certain substances that are produced by the nerve cell and the information is transmitted along the length of the nerve.

After the action potential, the original distribution has to be reinstated, sodium has to be pumped out of the cell and potassium back in. An enzyme, also called potassium-sodium pump, is responsible for that and this enzyme's function is dependent on magnesium. You can see that in order for the nervous system to function properly, at least three Schüssler salts are required.

You have to bear in mind, however, that potassium has to be inside the cell in order to stabilise the resting potential. If you give your sports horse potassium at the wrong time, i.e. immediately before a stressful situation, you will only achieve the opposite effect, because the potassium is still located outside the cells.

The importance of potassium for the acid/base metabolism is discussed in a separate chapter, because too many acids in the food compromise the horse's well-being and performance. If there is insufficient potassium inside the cell, acids will increase and can only be eliminated through the kidneys once they have been transported out of the cell, and again potassium is necessary for that.

An electron-microscopic image of potassium chloride.

An electron-microscopic image of potassium phosphate. (Photo: Deutsche Homöopathie-Union)

No 4: Potassium chloride

Potassium chloride is the natural opponent of sodium chloride (No 8). Sodium chloride binds water in the body, which can help horses that sweat heavily, whereas potassium chloride promotes water elimination. It is indicated in cases of oedemas, for example after protein excess, and its use will achieve two ends: improved water secretion and prevention of protein-related acidity.

No 5: Potassium phosphate

In order to stabilise the nervous system I use No 5 potassium for the resting potential, and phosphate for the energy supply. By burning phosphate, the body creates glucose, which supplies energy. Potassium phosphate has also shown its worth in mild cases of heart disease. It does not have to be fully developed heart muscle damage, but even the smallest reduction in the performance of the heart will lead to a loss of strength.

An electron-microscopic image of potassium sulphate. (Photo: Deutsche Homöopathie-Union)

No 6: Potassium sulphate

The anion sulphate plays the essential role in the No 6. The outer layers of skin, hair and horn contain a lot of sulphur. That is perhaps why the devil with his cloven hoof in the fires of hell smells so badly of sulphur. Potassium sulphate is used for all skin and hoof problems. In cases of parasitic skin disease, however, the mixture will only act as a support, because the parasites need first to be attacked with specific medications.

No 7: Magnesium phosphate

Magnesium is a spasmolytic substance and is effective against cramps. Calcium release triggers the transition from nerve impulse to muscle contraction, and magnesium is a natural opponent, or antagonist, of calcium. Heart patients will know this well: unwanted muscle contractions can be avoided, which brings relief to an angina patient and also loosens muscle tension in

An electron-microscopic image of magnesium phosphate. (Photo: Deutsche Homöopathie-Union)

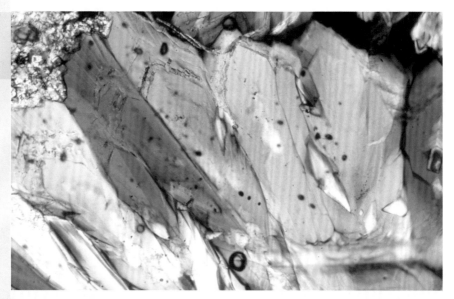

horses. Muscular problems that are caused by badly fitted tack or an inexperienced rider can be alleviated with magnesium phosphate. In cases of the dreaded tying-up syndrome, with serious tension of the rump muscles, magnesium phosphate can stop its development when only mild, or in severe cases helps to relieve the symptoms until the vet arrives and supports the treatment.

No 8: Sodium chloride

In human medicine, No 8 has lost its former importance because, unlike in past times, there is no lack of sodium in our diet any more. Indeed we often use too much sodium chloride as salt for cooking. Our horses, though, do not add salt to their feed, but when they sweat with exercise or excitement they lose a lot of sodium. The loss cannot be compensated with biochemical remedies alone, and salt or salt supplements are essential. The biochemical remedies improve the distribution and absorption of sodium. In the event of a problem with water distribution or dehydration, No 8 is indicated.

No 9: Sodium phosphate

Schüssler's thoughts about No 9 were ahead of their time. Knowledge in this area at that time was limited and mostly wrong. The Arrhenius hypothesis, which states that cations are alkaline and anions are acidic, was popular, but that is not quite true and led to many erroneous theories in medical publications. Only since Broenstedt's revised explanation in the 1920s have we known that the dissolved

An electron-microscopic image of sodium chloride. (Photo: Deutsche Homöopathie-Union)

An electron-microscopic image of sodium phosphate. (Photo: Deutsche Homöopathie-Union)

No 10: Sodium sulphate

Sodium sulphate, also known as Glauber's salt, is widely used as a laxative and is also suited for use in horses. If you are absolutely sure that the cause of a colic is not a blockage or twisted gut, sodium sulphate can help stimulate intestinal function.

No 11: Silicea

Silicea is a classical remedy for all connective tissue problems, i.e. tendons, ligaments, discs, joint cartilage and capsules, and also the soft tissue parts of bones. Plants that are used in medicine for similar indications all have a very high silicea content. Conventional medicine refused to acknowledge silicea, or silicon dioxide, as one of the essential minerals. It was not until a

hydrogen anion H^+ defines acidity. Sodium phosphate, according to Schüssler, was the classical substance to buffer aggressive acids. Based on our modern knowledge, No 5 (potassium phosphate) seems a better choice. More about that in the next chapter (page 43).

An electron-microscopic image of sodium sulphate. (Photo: Deutsche Homöopathie-Union)

An electron-microscopic image of silicea.
(Photo: Deutsche Homöopathie-Union)

thorough study carried out by the University of San Diego in the 1990s that silicea was proven to be vital for bone development and the production of collagen.

There are clues that our ancestors in the stone ages used stone meal, silicea, as a valuable medicine. One could easily imagine a scenario in which these early people damaged their backs while moving enormous rocks to build tumuli, and then scraped the precious medicine off the same rocks as treatment.

A sufficient supply of silicea is essential for free and supple movement.
(Photo: Slawik)

An electron-microscopic image of calcium sulphate. (Photo: Deutsche Homöopathie-Union)

No 12: Calcium sulphate

In biochemical literature, sometimes twelve and sometimes eleven tissue salts are mentioned. Schüssler placed this salt at the end of his list and later removed it, because he no longer considered it essential. However, it was then already well established and has been used ever since. Due to the sulphate component, it is mainly prescribed for treating abscesses, boils and fistulas.

Supplements

The so-called supplements were not of Schüssler's making. They were created by a commercially minded Mr Schöpwinkel around the time of the First World War, who had set up a lucrative trade near Dusseldorf offering various health and sexual enhancement remedies. Schöpwinkel was very much into esotericism and called his idea "the polar biochemistry as global law".

Below is a list of the currently recognised supplements in the order determined by the Biochemical Union:

The 12 supplements

No 13: potassium arsenate
No 14: potassium bromide
No 15: potassium iodide
No 16: lithium chloride
No 17: manganese sulphate
No 18: calcium sulphurate
No 19: copper arsenate
No 20: potassium aluminium
No 21: zinc chloride
No 22: calcium carbonate
No 23: sodium bicarbonate
No 24: arsenic iodide

Some more substances have entered the elite circle of Schüssler salts, although they have nothing to do with Schüssler any more. The Swiss company Pflüger even has a No 25 (aurum chloride) and No 26 (selenium) on their list. It is fascinating to observe

Some supplements have a beneficial effect on the immune system and also lead to a healthy, shiny coat.
(Photo: Slawik)

how cleverly and successfully a trace element as potentially toxic as selenium was marketed and has gained an albeit tentative scientific reputation.

Only a few of these supplements are actually useful, because they add another essential trace element to the existing remedies. Everyone has different priorities but I consider the elements manganese (manganese sulphate, No 17), copper (copper arsenate, No 19) and zinc (zinc chloride, No 21) helpful. Manganese is important for a quick metabolism of the lactate that is produced during muscle contraction after the oxygen has been depleted. Zinc increases the elimination of acids from the body and, like copper, has a beneficial effect on the immune system.

However, Schüssler would be mortified about some of the supplements. Numbers 13 (potassium arsenate), 14 (potassium bromide) and 15 (potassium iodide) are not about potassium, which is already available in the form of Nos 4, 5 and 6, but about their partners arsenic, bromide and iodine, all of which are highly toxic and have to be used with great caution. Numbers 22 (cal-cium carbonate) and 23 (sodium bicarbonate) are acidic combinations, and Schüssler was strictly against their use.

Biochemical ointments

Biochemical ointments were not Schüssler's idea; they were designed much later. They are particularly popular in human medicine for their cosmetic value, which is beyond the scope of this book.

It is unlikely that the minerals in these creams penetrate all the layers of the skin to have systemic effects in the blood and organs, although the ointments are certainly effective on the skin. However, most equine problems that affect the skin require conventional medication, for example creams and lotions against fungal infections or mites, or disinfectants.

Therefore, I do not believe there are many indications for ointments in horses. In the late stages of a healing wound, No 11 (silicea) can help minimise scar development.

Extreme physical demands deplete available oxygen in the muscle quickly, which leads to high concentrations of detrimental lactate. (Photo: Slawik)

The acid–base imbalance performance stopper
Acids make you ill

There is a saying in German: "Sour makes you happy." That is certainly not so acids make you ill, as we can see with our oceans, rivers, forests and fields. Acid–base imbalances also limit the best performance of human or animal athletes. Performance is directly linked to the ability of blood and metabolism to buffer acids.

During maximum exercise, a muscle will quickly use up the available oxygen through aerobic burning, and will then depend on the anaerobic energy supply. This process produces

Specific training can help the body to buffer acids in the blood better.
(Photo: Slawik)

lactate that is only slowly converted back to glucose. If anaerobic energy depletion continues, the lactate concentration rises more and more, and will finally lead to a break-down in performance. When this happens, a racehorse that seems in excellent shape, leading the field, can suddenly fall back because the accumulation of lactate stops its muscles working properly.

Training not only prepares the heart, lungs and muscles, it also improves the ability of the metabolism to buffer and eliminate developing acids. An enzyme that turns lactate back into glucose is responsible for the process.

The enzyme's nucleus contains manganese, the biochemical supplement No 17. Elimination through the kidneys—the only way out—depends on another enzyme, which requires the trace element zinc, No 21, for its function. Buffering of acids involves large concentrations of proteins, bicarbonates and phosphate in the blood. The aim of training is also to increase the amounts of enzymes and buffering substances in the blood.

Breathing helps to stop the increase of acids in the blood stream. We have known since the 1920s that the hydrogen anion H^+ determines acidity, and bicarbonates, HCO_{3^-}, define a base.

The acid–base balance is controlled firstly by the acidic hydrogen (H+) and then the alkaline bicarbonate (HCO3-) becoming carbonic acid (H2CO3). In order to transport the bicarbonate that is in the blood stream out of the body, it then has H2O taken away from it, which is eliminated through the kidneys and skin and the remaining CO2 is expelled from the lungs.

$$H^+ + CO_3\text{-} \rightleftharpoons H_2CO_3 \rightleftharpoons CO_2 + H_2O$$

When mixing both together we get carbonic acid, H_2CO_3, which again dissolves into H_2O and CO_2, water and carbon dioxide. The horse's breathing rate will increase in order to expel the carbon dioxide, it sweats profusely and will produce plenty of urine.

The breathing is able to prevent the blood pH from falling down to acidic levels. However, with every acidic ion, an alkaline cation will be eliminated too. The blood pH will remain constant but the buffer capacity will decrease rapidly, and the ability to prevent the lactate build-up in the muscles will eventually be exhausted. The higher the buffer capacity, the longer an athlete can produce energy from anaerobic processes.

I was involved in a research programme and in the development of a relatively simple measuring method, which for the first time would determine the buffer capacity under the influence of lactate build-up. The method of determining the buffer capacity in human medicine is known as the "Jörgensen method" and could also provide us with important clues about the fitness levels of horses.

Do not forget: it is not only the racehorse and marathon-runner who are athletes. An old person suffering from anaemia, circulation problems, heart insufficiency or asthma constantly reaches the limits of their strength, and their muscles quickly get into an anaerobic situation due to the lack of available oxygen. Improving the buffer capacity therefore not only helps your horse, but might also help your grandmother, who perhaps helps to pay for your hobby.

Common diseases and their treatment

Where salts can help

The horse is a moving animal, and we take advantage of this by using it as a sports animal. It has to run faster than any others; has to jump as high as it can; it has to bend and stretch, collect and extend, always trying its best to understand its rider's often misleading aids; and all this with often badly fitted saddles, shoes and bits, and a badly seated rider with spurs, stick and an iron hand, making it near impossible for the horse to enjoy its work. Sore and tense muscles, joint damage, back problems and resulting vices are not surprising.

A different trainer, rider, yard, saddle or farrier is often more effective than treatments, ointments, injections or drugs. Polite as I am, by using the word "often" I have given you the chance to blame others of course you are an exception.

If we want to use biochemical drugs, in order to find the correct treatment we have to look at the symptoms as well as the cause. It is not enough to have a quick fix of the acute problem. Unless we eliminate the underlying cause, the old situation will recur quickly.

Remedies 1, 2, 3, 7 and 11 are the classic choices for problems with the musculo-skeletal system, Nos 9 and 10 for the metabolism, Nos 6 and 12 for the skin, Nos 5 and 7 for the nervous system, and Nos 4 and 8 for the waterworks. Once you have learned the specific effect of each medication, you will understand why and when a remedy is indicated.

Musculo-skeletal system

chronic arthritis

Chronic arthritis is a degenerative condition of joints, and is different from acute arthritis, which is an inflammatory disease. The slow degeneration of joint cartilage can lead to a secondary inflammatory process, which is very painful. The veterinary surgeon usually treats arthritis with anti-inflammatory drugs (corticosteroids, or nonsteroidal anti-inflammatory drugs). The inflammation will then improve and the pain goes away, but the weak structure of the joint will remain. With biochemistry, we prefer medication that supports the natural inflammatory process, for example ferrum phosphate (No 3).

Cartilage is a substance that is continually renewed, which is a blessing for all arthritis patients. Problems can occur, however, when the rate of cell death is higher than that of cell regeneration. The trace element silicea (No 11) determines the quality and amount of newly formed cartilage.

Arthritic changes in horses happen predominantly in the fore legs (knee, fetlock and coffin joint) but changes to hip and stifle joints can occur too.

Many factors can play a role when a horse does not want to cooperate. Before using medication, you should check thoroughly, for example, the saddle, the shoes and the ability of the rider.
(Photo: Slawik)

A mad moment in the field can have serious consequences on landing, a small bone or cartilage fragment could splinter off and lead to further problems. (Photo: Slawik)

Arthritis of the hocks also develops frequently, and is called bone spavin.

Bone chips

A joint that is over-stressed can sustain injuries in which small cartilage or bone fragments, called bone chips, splinter off, and these then move freely within the joint capsule. Often, these chips do not cause any problems whatsoever, but when the chip gets trapped between the joint surfaces it can suddenly cause severe pain. In these cases surgical removal of the chip is necessary. With small chips, one can wait and see if the fragment causes any problems, or is even absorbed by the body. Silicea (No 11) should be used supportively.

Foals and yearlings quite frequently sustain such injuries. They are often due to feeding or stable mismanagements, or are a result of genetic predisposition.

Growth plates

Growth plates are gaps in the bones near the joints, from where the long bones of children and foals continue to grow. The plates close when the body is fully developed, and they give an indication of when that will occur. Juvenile athletes often complain about pain near the joints, which is usually caused from over-stressing the bones before the growth plates are closed. A young horse should not be worked before the bones have grown fully and the plates are closed.

Schüssler stated in his first publication that silicea hardens the bones, which most likely referred to the closure of the growth plates. Number 11 is most indicated here, especially if other family members have experienced skeletal problems.

If other members of your foal's family have known skeletal problems, No 11 can support growth and prevent bone problems later in life. (Photo: Slawik)

Fractures

Bone fractures used to be a definite death sentence for a horse, but nowadays, many fractures can be healed with the help of nails, screws and casts. You have to bear in mind, however, that the cost of such treatment, and subsequent long periods of convalescence, can easily accumulate to more than the value of the horse. But what horse lover thinks in those terms?

Convalescence is a frightening time: the first weight-bearing after the surgery, the first walk, the first lungeing, the first hack, the first canter and competition... Each occasion is scary is the bone going to be strong enough?

Bone mass is fibrous tissue plus calcium. You should now be able to guess the treatment: silicea (No 11) and calcium phosphate (No 2). Be careful, however, with No 1 (calcium fluoride). It hardens the bone, but if given in too high a dose the bones becomes too hard and therefore brittle. Human medicine has shown that osteoporosis patients who were given conventional fluoride medication suffered more bone fractures than untreated patients, but the dosage of these preparations was much higher and indeed close to toxic limits.

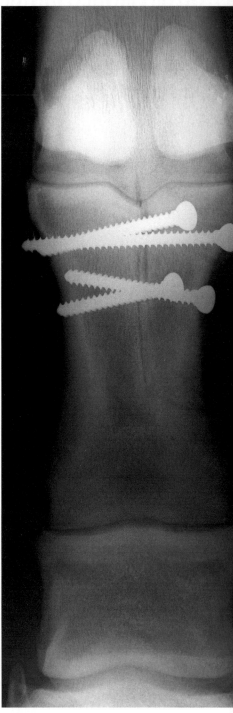

Modern surgical techniques can successfully repair many bone fractures in horses. Nos 11 and 2 support bone healing.
(Photo: Tierklinik Sottrum)

Laminitis

Laminitis is an inflammation of the layers in the hoof caused by over-stressing, incorrect feeding, or by the toxins of a retained afterbirth. An excess of proteins used to be thought of as the sole cause, but we know now that an overload of carbohydrates from grain or grass is mainly to blame. Intoxication, bad shoeing or a foot abscess can start off laminitis too.

A disturbed acid-base metabolism plays a significant role in the development of founders, the sinking of the pedal bone, and thus to permanent damage of the foot.

It makes sense to administer five tablespoons of sodium bicarbonate in the feed in the early phase of laminitis, and after a week change to No 9 (sodium phosphate). The obligatory anti-inflammatory (No 3) and connecting tissue (No 11) remedies should be given too. But nothing will work without a drastically reduced diet and good shoeing.

Acute laminitis causes severe pain that the horse tries to alleviate with this typical posture. (Photo: Slawik)

Each onset of laminitis is a serious emergency and needs to be treated immediately in order to avoid permanent damage. Veterinary treatment is most important, and biochemical remedies act purely as support.

Navicular disease is the classical disease of show jumpers because of the extreme forces acting on the foot that are imposed during landing and turning. (Photo: Slawik)

Navicular disease

One of the most common diseases of the skeletal system of riding horses is navicular disease. The navicular bone forms part of the coffin joint, and the deep flexor tendon runs over it to its attachment. A bursa lies like a cushion between tendon and bone in order to protect the bone. High forces on this area, especially during show

jumping and sharp turns, can lead to over-stressing, irritations, acute inflammations and finally permanent damage.

Other factors than such stress can be a cause as well, for example a very small hoof in relation to body size is a predisposing factor. Bad shoeing and trimming might create abnormal forces on the joints and lead to conformational problems. A good farrier and perhaps a year without shoes might be appropriate measures to stop this process at an early stage.

Biochemically we again use No 3 (ferrum phosphate) at an acute inflammatory stage, and No 11 (silicea) for cartilage. In order to improve loss of fluid from the bursa I would add No 8 (sodium chlorate). Once the acute lameness has improved, Nos 8 and 11 should still be given for another two to three months.

Patella luxation and upward fixation

Under some circumstances, the patella can slip from its normal position in the stifle joint or, more commonly, it locks and therefore prevents the hindleg from moving forward. This is not usually the case all the time; often it happens with the first step out of the stable, or when walking in a tight circle. Wear marks on the tip on the hoof can point towards this problem, because the limb is dragged over the ground. Bad conformation, neglected feet and weak muscles are predisposing factors for this condition. With age, it often improves.

Since this is predominantly a soft tissue problem, No 11 (silicea) is the treatment of choice while No 2 (calcium phosphate) helps strengthen the muscles. Corrective trimming or shoeing should be considered, as well as specific muscle training. If the problem cannot be resolved by these measures, surgical intervention is necessary. During such surgery, the patella ligament that locks the patella is cut.

Tying-up

The most dangerous form of muscle cramps is azoturia tying-up syndrome because numerous muscle cells are irreversibly damaged. Myoglobin, an oxygen binding cell-based protein, is released from the damaged cell and eliminated from the body in the urine, which turns dark brown. If too much myoglobin is being released, the kidneys can be damaged.

There are several types of azoturia; some are hereditary, and begin with subtle but then increasingly damaging muscle problems. The performance of these horses is very limited and you should not breed from them.

The acute and sporadic form of azoturia is also called tying-up syndrome because it usually happens in working horses after a couple of days of rest with unreduced amounts of hard feed. Even though this cause is nowadays viewed with caution, I would still recommend that you reduce the amount of hard feed significantly on days when your horse is not worked properly. I do not consider the question whether an excess of carbohydrates (grain) or protein acts as the trigger sufficiently answered. Oats are high in protein and it is better to feed them sparingly, because it is certain that an excess of protein reduces performance instead of improving it (see also acid–base imbalances, page 43)

The symptoms of azoturia usually appear after work. The strides become shorter and shorter, and the rump muscles are rock hard.

Ideas about treatment differ: some advise complete rest, others careful hand walking. In any case, the back should be kept warm. It is hard to say whether medication or prolonged resting periods lead to success in the end, but every slight sign of tying-up has to be taken seriously, and should your horse sweat and shake as well, you need to call the vet urgently.

Biochemically, the main treatment is No 7 (magnesium phosphate), ten tablets or more of D3 rather than D6. Conventional magnesium preparations given by intramuscular injection also help. In order to stabilise the acid–base metabolism I use either No 9 (sodium phosphate) or No 5 (potassium phosphate), based on recent research into acid–base imbalances. I would also treat horses with azoturia for three months with the biochemical supplements No 17 (manganese sulphate) and No 21 (zinc chloride) to support the many enzymes responsible for elimination of lactate from the body.

Muscular tension

No matter what you use your horse for, all training has to be based on trust.

Your horse has to be accustomed to saddle and rider, and ridden with understanding and patience. Mistakes in this early phase will lead to problems between horse and rider that are difficult to overcome later. Every lesson should start with loosening exercises. If your horse is forced too early and too quickly, its muscles will tense up.

Tension can also stem from underlying joint problems. It is not always easy to determine whether a horse is lame, or just stiff. In any case, a tense muscle uses energy and oxygen, hurts the horse and compromises its performance and willingness to work. The rider will not enjoy it, and neither will the horse.

The most important part of the therapy is to recognise and if possible eliminate the cause. Biochemically, Nos 5 (potassium phosphate) and 7 (magnesium phosphate) are indicated. Every muscular tension has a nervous involvement, and the resting potential of nerve cells is dependent on the potassium concentration in the cell.

The statement "potassium rather than valium" makes a good point. However, potassium only stabilises the resting potential if it reaches the inside of the cell, and in order to get there it needs magnesium hence also give No 7.

Capped hock

A capped hock is a visible swelling of the point of the hock. This swelling and inflammation is caused by mechanical influences, like knocking against a stable or lorry wall. The

A carefully designed training plan is the best prevention of muscular problems. (Photo: Slawik)

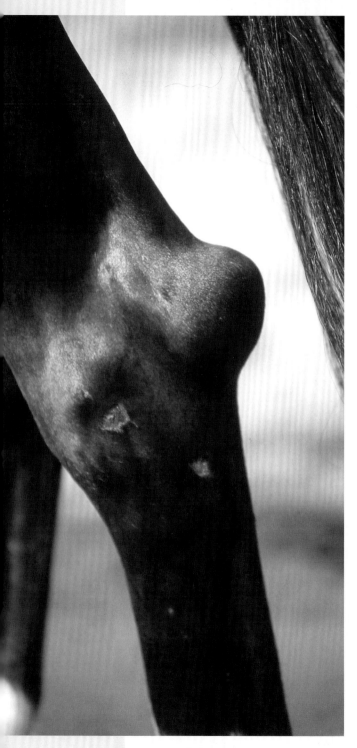

No 3 can help to cure acute capped hocks, and in order to strengthen the soft tissue, No 11 is indicated..
(Photo: Slawik)

horse is usually not lame even if the swelling is sore when pressed.

As a precaution, the sides in the lorry should be cushioned. In an acute case, No 3 (ferrum phosphate) is the medication of choice, and No 11 (silicea) can help strengthen the soft tissue. Number 8 (sodium chloride) is useful to reduce the swelling.

Tendon problems

Every rider dreads any tendon problems their horses could sustain, also called "bow" because of the bow-like shape of the injured tendon along the back of the canon bone.

The flexor tendons of both front legs are under extreme stress, especially during a fast gallop. In gallop, the horse lands on one front leg and the flexor tendons act as shock absorbers and suspension at the same time. Over-stressing an untrained tendon, or in the event of accidental wrong footing on the ground, the tendons can no longer withstand the forces.

You can compare it with trying to pull a vehicle, using a towrope. If you pull carefully with slowly increasing force you will be successful; however, if you suddenly pull a slack rope with great force, the rope will snap. When a horse gets tired, the muscle tone reduces and therefore the tendons slacken between the strong forces. Single fibres tear, or in the worst case the whole of the tendon ruptures.

Ruptures of single fibres are accompanied by bruising, inflammation and swelling. A careful owner will detect

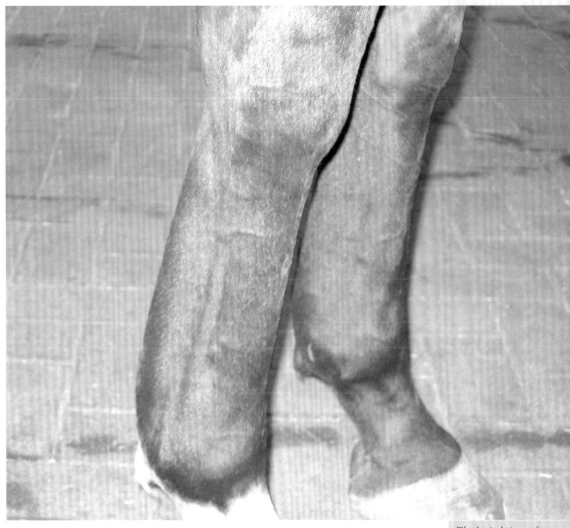

The classical picture of a tendon injury: the back of the canon bone is shaped like a "bow". (Photo: Jörgensen)

the first signs of the damage even before the swelling appears by carefully palpating the uplifted leg, and he will rest the horse. The recovery period is long and is more successful when the injury is detected early.

Racehorses frequently sustain tendon injuries because of the enormous pressure they are put under. These horses are sometimes retired early and sold, but can still make excellent pleasure horses and be fully fit for many years.

Ice packs and anti-inflammatory drugs can achieve temporary pain relief, but cannot heal the lesions by themselves and sometimes they merely mask the damage.

No 3 (ferrum phosphate) is effective again, as with all inflammations, and it does not mask the problem but supports the body's own healing power.

Tendons of sport horses have to withstand extreme forces—in order to avoid permanent damage a thorough check of the legs after hard exercise is important.
(Photo: Slawik)

Do not forget—an inflammation is not an illness, but the body's attempt to repair damage. The question arises whether it is always necessary and sensible to administer conventional anti-inflammatory drugs like corticosteroids or non-steroidals, or whether the supportive self-healing approach with No 3 might be better. Because tendons are built with collagen tissue No 11 (silicea) is useful here to improve tissue quality.

Withers and back problems

Back problems are usually closely linked to muscular tension and also to riding problems. Therefore, a thorough loosening phase is important at the beginning of every lesson. The spinal processes point away from each other when the back moves upwards and is arched, but when the spine is bent downwards and the spinal column becomes concave, the gaps between the processes narrow and they can even touch. This can lead to painful inflammations, called kissing spines, and if left untreated the horse can become unrideable.

A badly fitted saddle will cause tension, and a horse that has not learned to accept the rider trustfully will be resistant, which is uncomfortable for the rider. A well-ridden horse has a swinging and elastic back.

X-rays frequently reveal damage at an advanced stage and then it is most likely too late. Some X-ray changes, however, are not considered pathological and are harmless variations. X-ray studies of the backs of foals have shown variations of what is considered normal without any connected medical problems.

As treatment, a change in the training regime is important. The horse needs to be encouraged to stretch down in order to strengthen the back. Nos 5 and 7 help to relax and No 11 to strengthen the soft tissue.

Digestive system

Diarrhoea

Causes of diarrhoea in an adult horse are mainly feeding related. A drastic change in diet, for example, when turned out to pasture in spring, a change from hay to silage, or a different concentrate can upset the digestive system Treatment in this case is, of course, to readjust the diet.

As in humans, horses can suffer from stress-related diarrhoea too. You need to eliminate the cause of the stress and

A lush pasture without acclimatisation—a recipe for laminitis and diarrhoea.
(Photo: Slawik)

improve the horse's psychological well-being.

Antibiotic drugs can damage the physiological flora of the gut so much that it results in diarrhoea, but this should recover a few days after the treatment.

You should not wait too long, especially with foals, because with diarrhoea the body loses fluids as well as important minerals. Dehydration and circulation problems can occur—and the younger the foal, the more dangerous this is.

In chronic cases the vet can examine a faecal sample in order to check for infections of the gut.

Biochemically, No 8 (sodium chloride) binds water and can minimise dehydration and harden the faeces. In order not to disturb the sodium/potassium balance, I usually also add No 4 (potassium chloride).

In cases of severe diarrhoea the horse needs to be put on a drip, and minerals have to be replaced in concentrated form instead of as homeopathic doses.

Gastritis

Gastritis and stomach ulcers are increasingly common problems in horses. It is well documented in humans that stress can lead to ulcers. Why should this not happen to a horse?

If stress is the cause, it needs to be reduced by improving stable management and work, or changing the dietand of course consider No 5 (potassium phosphate). Also remember that

internal parasites can cause gastritis. Regular worming is essential.

Colic

Acute colic can be anything from a bit of wind to a complete blockage, but sometimes the assumed colic has completely different origins, such as a twisted uterus, kidney problems and many other dramatic conditions that require surgical intervention. Therefore, do not hesitate to call your vet at the very first signs of colic. Until the vet arrives, you can dissolve No 7 (magnesium phosphate) in warm water and squirt it into the horse's mouth.

Choke

Feed materials like dry sugar beet and nuts sometimes swell before they reach the stomach, and block the oesophagus, while hay and straw eaten hastily without being chewed can cause a blockage as well. The horse chokes and coughs up foamy food particles that run from mouth and nostrils.

This can go unnoticed if the horse is being transported and all you find are food and saliva traces on the floor.

In acute cases, spasmolytic drugs administered by the vet will relieve the cramps. Oral drugs are not indicated because of the blockage. Horses that are prone to develop choke can be treated with No 7 (magnesium phosphate), to alleviate and prevent cramps.

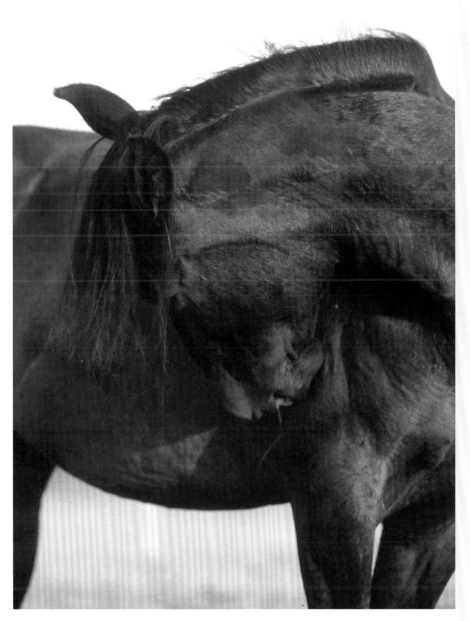

As soon as you detect signs of colic—like turning the head towards the stomach—the vet needs to be called.
Until he or she arrives, No 7 can bring relief.
(Photo: Slawik)

Worms

Certainly worms are no indication for homeopathic or biochemical drugs, even if you are sceptical of the obviously poisonous (for worms) conventional treatment. Because we keep horses in small, fenced-in fields or in stables, and not on wide open steppes like their ancestors, we will fight a continuous battle against worms and their larvae. Horses should be treated four times a year with the appropriate medication, depending on season and type of worms. Enquire with your veterinary surgeon. Supportively, No 10 (sodium sulphate) should be given.

Teeth problems

Babies cry when their first teeth appear. Foals are more tolerant, but if they or any young horse shows any teething problems No 2 (calcium phosphate) will help.

Like humans, horses can develop dental caries, but it rarely causes problems because horses' teeth continually wear and grow. Caries will only cause pain if the decay develops faster than the teeth are worn, in which case treatment becomes necessary. If a nerve is inflamed, No 3 (ferrum phosphate) is effective. Number 1 (calcium fluoride) should be given to horses that are prone to caries because it hardens the tooth substance.

Sharp points along the outside of the teeth need to be rasped. The points can damage the membrane of the mouth and cause inflammation. As a result, the horse will not eat properly any more because of the pain when chewing the food. In addition to urgent teeth rasping, No 3 (ferrum phosphate) is the remedy of choice.

Respiratory system

Allergic bronchitis

An allergy can be a life-threatening condition, because repeated exposure to the allergenic agent can suddenly turn into an anaphylactic shock, with breakdown of the circulation. Luckily, not all allergies are that severe.

Allergic bronchitis, like all allergies, develops because of an exaggerated response from the immune system to the presence of foreign proteins in the body. Often, reactions to foreign substances and chemicals are described as allergies, but are no more than an incompatibility, without the dangerous potential of turning into an anaphylactic shock.

The symptoms of an allergy are caused by the release of predominantly histamine from mast cells. The mast cells are loaded with histamine and their membranes can be stabilised with calcium and zinc, therefore No 2 (calcium phosphate) and the supplement No 21 (zinc chloride) can minimise or even prevent the effects. All horses, but especially those suffering from allergic bronchitis, need plenty of fresh air, dust-free feed and proper, regular exercise.

Infectious bronchitis

All infectious diseases of the airway, whether upper airways, larynx or gut-

A horse suffering from allergic bronchitis needs plenty of fresh air at all times.
(Photo: Slawik)

Auscultation of the airways reveals the extent of the damage. (Photo: Slawik)

tural pouches are affected, including bronchitis or even pneumonia, have the same underlying cause: the immune system is unable any longer to prevent the manifestation of bacteria or viruses. Therefore, the basis of every treatment is to stimulate the defence system, unless the veterinary surgeon advises to the contrary.

Infectious bronchitis usually starts with a viral infection, most commonly influenza, herpes or rhino virus. Antibiotics such as penicillin are ineffective against viruses. Because of the subsequently weakened immune system, bacteria, e.g. streptococci, can then cause a secondary infection. Only then are antibiotics indicated.

Fungal spores, for example from aspergillus, can also manifest themselves on the damaged membranes. It is often difficult to identify them exactly, even with microscopic analysis of bronchial fluid.

Endoscopy allows visual examination of the airways, but thorough disinfection of the endoscope is crucial so that the instrument does not transmit any viruses to other horses.

The symptoms of bronchitis are classic and will alone confirm the diagnosis: coughing, raised temperature (above 38°). Each long-lasting bronchitis episode bears the risk of permanently damaging the bronchi, leading to the development of chronic bronchitis, allergies or even emphysema.

A horse with bronchitis should be rested for at least two to three weeks, to allow the immune system to strengthen. Exercise will lead to increased and deeper breathing, and bacteria will thereby reach other parts of the lungs.

A cough without fever can be a sign of infestation with worm larvae in the lungs, but dust will irritate the lungs too and the finer the particles, the deeper down they penetrate. Last but not least, certain gases irritate the airways as well, most commonly ammonia rising from deep bedding.

No 3 (ferrum phosphate) and No 21 (zinc chloride) help support the immune system. Number 2 (calcium phosphate) is indicated as prevention of allergies and No 7 (magnesium phosphate) if the cough is connected with spasms.

Emphysema

In the course of allergic bronchitis, the delicate alveoli deep down in the lungs become more and more damaged. Many of these fine bubbles burst and converge, thus reducing the surface area that is used for oxygen exchange between air and blood. Emphysema develops, causing permanent damage because the broken down tissue cannot be renewed. It depends on the extent of the illness whether such a horse can still be ridden.

The connected increase in blood flow resistance will weaken the heart, although a weak heart can also lead to emphysema and it is not always easy to establish the primary cause.

You can try and alleviate the condition biochemically with No 2 (calcium phosphate), as it eases allergic symptoms and also supports the heart. If the vet has prescribed the heart medication digitalis, No 2 will increase the effectiveness of the digitalis. Number 5 (potassium phosphate) is also energising for the heart and circulation.

Roaring

Roaring, also called whistling, is a distinct noise of inspiration, which increases with exercise. Constricted airflow also affects the performance negatively, especially during strenuous work. Diagnosis is confirmed by endoscopy.

Young horses often suffer from a transient inflammation of the pharynx that I would treat with No 3 (ferrum phosphate), but usually roaring is due to a paralysed nerve that affects the opening of the windpipe. In this case, any therapeutic success is unlikely. Number 5 (potassium phosphate) can be tried in order to stabilise the nerves and is best in combination with No 7 (magnesium phosphate).

Nose and lung bleeds

Bloody discharge from the nostrils of a racehorse is usually caused by bleeding from the lungs. The extreme workload of the airways leads to small ruptures of blood vessels and alveoli. Many of these bleeds will go unnoticed because they are too small for the blood to reach the nostrils, but they still cause a drop in performance. American researchers estimate that about 60 per cent of all racehorses suffer from lung bleeds. Attempts to lower the blood pressure with diuretic drugs have not proved successful and are in any case banned in Europe. Number 11 (silicea) can be tried because of its strengthening effect on connecting tissue.

Hoof, skin, coat

External parasites

The most common external parasites are mites and fungi. It is most important to check for these properly and

The dreaded lung bleed of racehorses is a common problem that often goes unnoticed but leads to a drop in performance.
(Photo: Slawik)

consult the vet if in doubt. The therapy should be aimed at the parasitic agent, not the horse, and usually conventional medication is required. Biochemistry, however, can help to restore a healthy and resilient skin. Potassium sulphate (No 6) is helpful with all skin diseases. Skin tissue contains a lot of sulphur and potassium sulphate speeds up regeneration.

Hoof problems

Small superficial cracks in the hoof wall are usually harmless, but they should be regularly checked to make sure that they do not get longer or worse deeper. They should be kept clean, because an infection deep in the foot can have severe consequences.

If the crack starts at the bottom, the farrier can help. Good shoeing minimises the pressure on the crack and the tear can grow out. Cracks in the coronary band are more serious because of potential damage to horn-producing tissue.

The idea of stopping further cracking by cutting a grove across the end of the gap is now obsolete. The structure of the horn capsule is not like a wooden board that simply tears along its fibres. Additional grooves will only damage the hoof further.

A sufficient supply of all minerals and trace elements is absolutely essential. Biochemically, No 6 (potassium sulphate) helps as well as the vitamin biotin.

A horse that is very prone to hoof cracks might have a hereditary condition and you should consider this before breeding from such an animal.

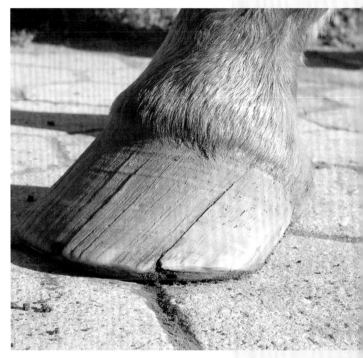

Sufficient supply of minerals and trace elements is important for a good horn quality. (Photo: Bosse)

Lack of hygiene in the stable, the field or paddock is the most common cause of mud fever. (Photo: Slawik)

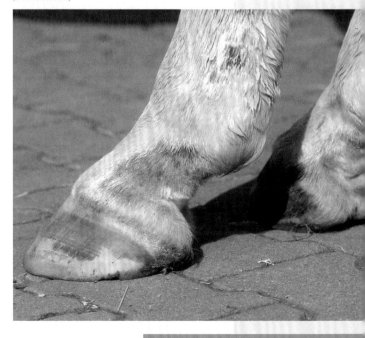

The agonising itching connected with sweet itch significantly compromises the welfare of a horse. (Photo: Slawik)

Mud fever

Mud fever is an inflammation located in the fetlock area that is brought about by dirty bedding and fields. Horses' lower legs should be dried with a soft towel after hosing or when coming in from a wet paddock. Horses with long feathers are more often affected, and sometimes the feathers have to be clipped off in order to apply cream and allow air to get to the skin.

Creams containing zinc and additionally supplement No 21 (zinc chloride) can help quickly. Wounds might have to be disinfected before applying the cream in order to avoid spreading the infection. And do not forget to use the towel.

Sweet itch and allergic skin diseases

Many causes for sweet itch have been suggested, but there is no doubt that biting midges are involved.

Conventional veterinary treatment is usually based on drugs containing cortico-steroids which of course suppress the immune system to a certain degree.

The best therapy is to protect the horse from the midges. This is not easy to do and it would be fantastic to have some bushes around the fields that deter midges and flies. Turning out at night protects from flies, but midges are still active in darkness. Rugs and fly masks are more effective, but they are uncomfortable in the heat of summer. Lotions and sprays do not last that long, especially when the horse sweats, and they all contain toxic substances.

The ideal solution has yet to be found.

The intense itching causes the horse to rub constantly and therefore damage the skin even more. It is caused partly by the insect toxin and partly by released histamine from mast cells. Zinc has a stabilising influence on cell membranes and therefore I recommend for all itchy skin problems a combination of zinc chloride (No 21) and calcium phosphate (No 2).

The risk of developing allergies is particularly high in cases of a disturbed mineral balance. The food should supply sufficient amounts of the elements calcium, potassium, magnesium and sodium. Examining occasional soil, hay and hard feed samples is recommended to ensure that requirements are met. If in doubt, mineral licks can be offered, or vitamin and mineral supplements can be added to the hard feed.

The most effective means of treating an allergy is to remove the allergen from the horse's environment, but often that is impossible. We are left with stabilising mast cell membranes to minimise histamine release, with Nos 2 and 21.

In the case of anaphylactic shock — and every allergy can turn into one — the vet alone can help with emergency drugs (cortico-steroids and adrenalin).

Thrush

Thrush is a bacterial infection in the frog of the foot. Again, prevention is better than cure. Daily hoof care, thorough and gentle cleaning of the frog, daily mucking out, no deep litter bedding, dry paddock etc …

Mineral licks should always be available—horses know when they need them. (Photo: Slawik)

If thrush develops, however, the farrier should trim off the decayed horn as far as possible. The remaining horn should be disinfected daily. Exercise the horse lightly on soft ground, because this will stimulate new horn growth.

I recommend the classical anti-inflammatory remedy No 3 (ferrum phosphate) and also No 12 (calcium sulphate). With all skin or horn problems, one of the sulphate combinations, No 6 or No 12, should be added, because sulphur is an important component of all skin cells.

Nerves and psyche

Ataxia

Ataxia is a condition that affects the coordination of movement. The horse appears to be lame or drunk, cannot lift its legs properly, stumbles and drags its toes. The cause can be brain damage, but usually it originates from an injury to the neck vertebrae after a fall or tumble. This subsequently leads to swelling or inflammation of the spinal cord and damage to the nerves. Interaction between the cord and external nerves is disturbed.

Anti-inflammatory drugs help at an early stage. Chiropractitioners or osteopaths can try to improve the positioning of the vertebrae, but that carries some risks and should be left to an experienced person.

No 3 (ferrum phosphate) and No 4 (potassium chloride) are indicated, and in chronic cases also No 11 (silicea).

Nervousness

It is frightening how many people believe that drugs are able to help humans (even children, and now also animals) to become confident, self-aware, psychologically stable, fearless and happy. Most of these drugs were discovered accidentally because certain wormers, older tuberculosis drugs, dyes or fuels triggered euphoria in people.

Over the years, the mechanisms of these drugs have been researched thoroughly and we know that all medications that are intended to treat mental problems are also able to create them when over-dosed.

Therefore, the regular use of psychopharmacological drugs in horses should be avoided, and if used at all, only be administered by a veterinary surgeon for short procedures. Even when loading a horse for the first time, which is certainly a stressful experience for the animal, patience is the best medication.

All tranquilizers are banned in competitions and racing, but the biochemical remedies Nos 4, 5 and 6, the potassium combinations, can be used. In particular No 5 does not suppress nerve functions like a tranquilizer, and it does not stimulate them either like anti-depressants. Number 5 merely stabilises the resting potential of nerves, which means that a nerve cell does not necessarily respond to incoming impulses. There is truth in the saying "potassium rather than valium".

Vices

Crib biting, weaving, pacing, pawing and kicking are what we call vices because they are stereotypical actions and they can drive owners mad. The cause, however, is usually found with the owner and not the horse. A horse that is meant to be outside running free is confined to a small stable for 23 hours a day, and often without companions. I must admit that I would go crazy too if I was locked in such a prison cell.

Has it lost its mind? All too often, some wonder drugs are given, instead of building trust and gently supporting your horse's psyche. (Photo: Slawik)

First of all, the stable management needs to be changed: more turn-out or exercise, more work, less stress, at least visual contact with other horses, more roughage instead of concentrate, and maybe toys in the stable. The three potassium combinations, Nos 4, 5 and 6, should be given as support.

The same remedies are indicated for stallions, sometimes also mares and geldings that turn against themselves when frustrated. Although a muzzle or collar can prevent self-mutilation to a certain degree, they will not solve the underlying psychological problem. Companions if possible but at least visual contact with other horses, and sufficient exercise, are the way forward. The use of psychopharmaceutical drugs or tranquilizers cannot be recommended.

Heart and circulation

Vascular problems

The most common vascular disease affecting horses is arteritis, an inflammation of arteries, predominantly in the intestinal system. Strongylus vulgaris larvae that move up the artery cause the disease. The inflammation of the vessel leads to thrombosis and narrowing of the lumen, and blood flow is restricted. In severe cases the arterial wall can begin to weaken and bulge outwards, creating a so-called aneurism, which might even burst and lead to a fatal bleeding. The inflammation and circulation disturbances also create colic-like pain. Regular worming is a good precaution.

After treatment, the damaged blood vessel usually heals and tightens again, like a scar. Number 11 (silicea) works here as support.

Heart disease

The heart is the central pump that provides circulation and therefore enables all muscular activity. If the heart does not function properly, performance is compromised. This does not necessarily mean that a horse cannot be ridden any more. Most horses do not have to do fast work but just gently hack across the countryside. The question of how significant a heart condition is depends on the level of required work.

Common conditions of humans, i.e. high blood pressure or angina, do not affect horses. More relevant are congenital valve problems, heart muscle damage after infections or with chronic lung disease and arrhythmias.

The horse owner usually first notices a reduced performance and increased breathing rate. It is advisable to have, besides a thermometer, a simple stethoscope in the stable, because it is often difficult to find a horse's pulse on the jaw or tail. Using a stethoscope, the heartbeat can be easily detected on the left-hand side between the fifth and sixth ribs.

The resting pulse of 28–40 beats per minute will increase drastically not only with exercise but also with fear and excitement, and therefore is not a reliable indicator of the condition of the horse. More indicative is the time it takes for the heart rate to settle back to normal again after exercise.

Many arrhythmias that are present when the horse is rested disappear with exercise. Because of the beneficial effect of potassium on the resting potential of nerve endings, No 5 (potassium phosphate) provides good support, as well as No 7 (magnesium phosphate) for relaxation. Potassium phosphate is also called a 'heart energiser'.

If the heart muscle is seriously weak and the horse develops a heart weakness, competing should no longer be considered. Turn out to pasture or light hacks, supported by No 5 (potassium phosphate) are often still possible for quite some time.

Most pleasure horses do not ever have to work hard, unlike this heavy horse. Heart conditions are therefore not always a serious problem. (Photo: Bosse)

Kidneys and urinary tract

Urinary retention

Some horses, geldings and stallions, more often than mares, have problems urinating. They position themselves to do so but it takes a long time until the urine actually passes, and sometimes it does not pass at all. Magnesium (No 7) has spasmolytic properties and should be given over several weeks.

Bladder infection

Persistent bacterial infections require antibiotic treatment. In mild or early cases and as supporting veterinary treatment, it is advisable to administer No 3 (ferrum phosphate), the classic anti-inflammatory remedy, in combination with the supplement No 21 (zinc chloride) which is important for many immunological functions.

Fertility

Missing cycles

During some years, all studs complain about problems with mares' cycles. Climatic influences seem to be the cause. It is now common practice to determine ovulation by checking the follicles regularly and sometimes to induce ovulation with hormone injec-

tions. If you prefer a more natural approach, however, and are happy to wait for the season to develop, a combination of No 21 (zinc chloride D6) and No 7 (magnesium phosphate D3) is the recommended choice.

Retained afterbirth

Some mares tend to retain the afterbirth, or produce it only very slowly. Parts of the placenta remaining in the uterus can lead to laminitis. If the afterbirth does not come out shortly after the birth, do not hesitate to call your vet, if he is not already present for the birth.

The vet will inject oxytocin to induce contractions. In the meantime, give your mare at least ten tablets of No 2 (calcium phosphate D3) dissolved in water directly into the mouth. Calcium increases the effect of oxytocin and with a bit of luck the problem will already have been resolved by the time the vet arrives.

Infertility of stallion

The mobility of sperm and their ability to travel towards the ovulated egg depends on the content of the prostrate fluid and this is dependent on a sufficient supply with the trace element zinc. Biochemically, the supplement No 21 (zinc chloride) is helpful.

It is not always easy to get a mare in foal Nos 7 and 21 can be supportive here. (Photo: Slawik)

Arrived: it can sometimes be helpful to support labour with No 2.
(Photo: Slawik)

Unless regular sperm analyses are being carried out, fertility problems will only show up after the breeding season. In order to improve the success rate in the following year, No 21 should be given during the whole autumn and winter.

Labour problems

As with a retained afterbirth, oxytocin is also responsible for inducing labour, and calcium phosphate (No 2) increa- ses contractions and speeds up the birth.

Do not forget though that the bio- chemical tablets only have a support- ive effect if the weak contractions are due to a serious calcium deficiency or old age. There are, of course, various other factors that can slow down the birth, for example a wrongly posi- tioned foal. In these cases, there can be fatal consequences if you just rely on natural remedies and do not call your vet immediately.

Appendix

The Biochemical Union and associated groups

Dr Schüssler's therapies encountered objections at first. Nevertheless, and as a riposte to his opponents, his satisfied patients formed a society in order to support and promote his methods. Workmen, traders and railway workers in Oldenburg founded the first Biochemical Union in 1885, and others followed quickly. These groups were disrupted during the two world wars and at times of inflation. Today, however, there are over 80 biochemical societies affiliated to the Biochemical Union of Germany (Biochemischer Bund Deutschlands e.V.). They hold lectures and seminars and produce literature to explain the biochemical principles.

The Biochemical Union also has a register of societies, biochemically practising doctors and homeopaths, as well as information about its work.

Schüssler tissue salts are available from various health food shops and pharmacies in the UK as well as through internet-based mail order, for example Barefoot Botanicals (http://www.barefoot-botanicals.com/tissue-salts.asp), or Planta (http://www.planta.co.uk/).

About the author

Hans-Heinrich Jörgensen has been a homeopath since 1962. During the 1970s, he developed a multi-mineral supplement for humans that is also widely used for animals. He was a member of the mineral and vitamin supplement section of the German State Health Department for many years. Today, he is vice chairman and consultant of the Biochemical Union.

His hobby, if you can call it a hobby, is breeding and training racehorses in Grossenkneten, south of Oldenburg, and he employs two jockeys and two junior members of staff for his 20 horses. He is also a member of the examination board for professional stud and yard managers (racing yards) in Nordrhein-Westfalen.

Contact email bio@nam.de

CADMOS
HORSE BOOKS

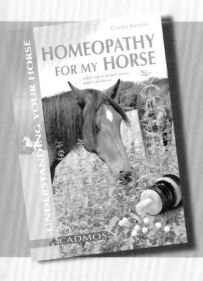

Claudia Naujoks
HOMEOPATHY FOR MY HORSE

Holistic help for the most common ailments and diseases

96 pages, illustrated
paperback

ISBN 978-3-86127-925-9
£ 9.95

Heike Gross
BEWARE POISON!

A horse-owner's guide to harmful and indigestible plants

32 pages, illustrated
paperback

ISBN 978-3-86127-950-1
£ 4.95

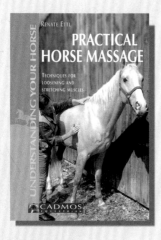

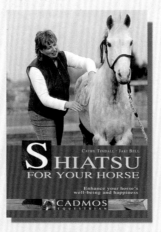

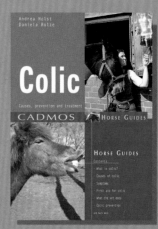
Renate Ettl
PRACTICAL HORSE MASSAGE

Techniques for loosening and stretching muscles

96 pages, illustrated
paperback

ISBN 978-3-86127-903-7
£ 9.95

Cathy Tindall/Jaki Bell
SHIATSU FOR YOUR HORSE

Enhance your horse's well-being and happiness

144 pages, illustrated
hardbound with jacket

ISBN 978-3-86127-915-0
£ 19.95

Andrea Holst/Daniela Bolze
COLIC

Causes, prevention and treatment

32 pages, illustrated
paperback

ISBN 978-3-86127-945-7
£ 4.95

Cadmos Books c/o Vicky Tischer · 13 The Archers Way · Glastonbury BA6 9JB
Phone +44 (0) 1458 834 229
To order online, please visit: **www.cadmos.co.uk**

CADMOS